SILENCE SPEAKS

Volume Three
Consciousness

GIAN MICHAEL SIMMONS

Copyright © 2021 Gian Simmons
All rights reserved.
ISBN: 978-1-955638-00-5

DEDICATION

Silence Speaks will be available in four volumes and released on the same day. I wrote Silence Speaks for all those that live amongst us and call ourselves human, including ourselves. This book is for all those that know that they are human and inhabit the earth but wonder where, in the world, did I come from? They live amongst us. They're even in our body. In fact, when we look ourselves in the mirror, something extra-terrestrial is looking right at them, but sometimes we wonder, not only where did I come from but if I am human, at all. We live amongst each other. We breathe the same air. May we uncover the commonality and oneness of all. May we see that we are One. We are Love.

CONTENTS

ACKNOWLEDGMENTS

The contents of this book are part of a vast collection of many unreleased, private writings, and conversations with the Voice that speaks in silence. I dedicate the inspiration to release this book to the Voice that speaks in silence; for using me as a vessel to share this message of love with the world. This Voice has shown me that Love should be your sword and shield. Love is a golden characteristic of the strong and brave. Love conquers all things. I am grateful to be the ambassador of this important message. I also give honor and thanks to the Mother, the Father, my parents, my son, family, friends, strangers, children of Love, and extra-terrestrials. Special acknowledgement to my mother who has gone on to the stars

ABOUT THE AUTHOR

About Gian Michael Simmons Productions

Gian Michael Simmons is a follower of Jesus Christ, proud father, to Isaiah, and an active philanthropist. He has worked in the Wealth Management industry for the last two decades. Gian recently retired a success-ful 19-year financial career to focus on **Gian Michael Simmons Productions.**

Since turning his passion into a profession, Gian started **Gian Michael Simmons Productions, a**

multi-conglomerate business exchange of enterprises, which includes books, websites, online businesses, publishing, faith, and more. He has written prolifically and is constantly exploring new themes, genres, and ideas. He enjoys challenging himself and mastering his talents. Gian is a very active writer and writes daily. Many of his writings have been completed within minutes and requiring minimalistic editing. It's very common to find him sitting down at his desk putting the opening words to a new book, poem, or story on paper or a daily motivational social media post. He credits his gifts to his consciousness and relationship with God. It's incredibly hard work, but he's never happier than when he follows the Father, the Voice that speaks in silence and love.

The movement has begun! **Silence Speaks Love Liberates**

Silence Speaks and **Love Liberates** are movements combined with business projects and followed by a Multi-Book-Volume Series, over 100 pages in each volume, to connect you with God. **Silence Speaks Jesus Saves book is a standalone book and not a series volume book.** The series are designed for one to read in any order, as each multi-dimensional book has a different focus matter of discussion and flows with the overall theme of Silence Speaks and Love Liberates. For committed and advanced readers, you may read the series in the order as follows as each following volume presents a journey to God and additional aroma to the **feature books, which are <u>highlight books for all readers</u>. The feature book for Gian Michael Simmons Productions is "Silence Speaks Jesus Saves".** <u>I would highly suggest that all to read this volume</u>. **For the Silence Speaks Volume Series, the feature book** is **Silence Speaks Volume Seven: I AM THAT I AM, Gian Michael Simmons.** Again, all books may be read in any order. The focus and contents of each book may be found in each book description. Additionally, all projects are described in mission statements.

Repent. Seek ye the kingdom of heaven is at hand Jesus holds the keys to salvation

Gian attained his bachelor's degree from the State University of New York at Albany, where he served as a student president for over three years.

Gian was the first college graduate in his family. He was proud of the opportunity to encourage others. He was a very active student-leader and he served as President for three consecutive years and received the President's Undergraduate Leadership Award, the highest prestigious recognition, for each of those years. During Gian's freshman year, he wrote and directed a play and filled the audience. He donated the proceeds to a local charity. This would become the event that would land Gian the office of presidency. During his leadership at Albany, Gian galvanized the students and leaders, had many landmark events, and left a historical lasting impact felt throughout generations of students, past and current. Gian always committed his life's mission to developing relationships, creativity, leadership, diversity and equality, community service, philanthropy, and being a seeker of the kingdom of heaven.

During Gian's leadership years at the University at Albany, he represented the students with leaders such as the Late- Coretta Scott King, the- Late Betty Shabazz, Hillary Clinton, the Late-Congressman John Lewis, the Late- Maya Angelou, Dr. Sonia Sanchez, Saul Williams, Chuck D, Professor Griff, Tommy Hilfiger, the Late- Dr. Carson Carr Jr., Dr. Marcia Sutherland, Dr. James Turner, Cornel West, Jay Z, Diddy, Wyclef Jean, just to name a few. Gian is very talented, loves to create, and rise in leadership. In college, Gian planned many events. One event that he's most proud about is founding the first Capital District Hip Hop Conference attended by many from all over the world. Gian wrote the blueprint for the 3-day conference, which included several events such as workshops, keynote speakers, panel discussions, poetry event, hip hop show and party, dinners, and fashion show. Gian enjoys being a leader and providing opportunities of progressive growth for man and equal opportunity.

Gian has always remained an active member in his community. In his spare time, he enjoys reading and writing. He also loves to cook. At a young age, Gian would ask his mother to buy him books instead of toys.

His favorite book was the Bible and dictionary and he loved to learn new words daily. Gian has been writing from a very young age and enjoys exercising various writing styles. His dream is to write movies. Gian enjoys being a student of the engagements of words and characters. Writing has always been a hobby for Gian. Gian is a student of wisdom, knowledge, and a seeker of higher truths. Gian enjoys maintaining an intimate relationship with God through His Son, Jesus Christ. Gian enjoys reading the Holy Bible, studying text and verses, learning from the parables and stories, the threshing floor of prayers, learning obedience and the laws of God, studying the prophets, and allowing the text to clothe himself as coats of skin and armor of protection. Gian has always heard the calling and enjoys walking with God.

Gian is also excited to announce the start the foundations of his non-profit organization called "**Love Liberates Inc. Nonprofit**". A portion of this book's proceeds will go to help start this charitable project that he's very excited about. The mission of Love Liberates is to restore the hopes and joys of life, to motivate and encourage others, to foster mentorship, meditation group, inner city community services, and homeless outreach.

Gian also created a social media website with full-service features for a safe place for people to fellowship, join groups and network, learn new things, expand in wisdom and understanding, be entertained with engaging writings, blogs, and podcasts, shop with free worldwide shipping, and more.

You may find **Gian Michael Simmons Productions** and **Love Liberates Non-Profit** at www.gianmichael-simmons.com and follow Gian's social media pages for updates. Gian can be found @GianMichaelSimmons on Facebook, LinkedIn, Instagram, WordPress and @ GianMSimmons on Twitter. Stay tuned!

Bookmark and Become a Member
WWW.GIANMICHAELSIMMONS.COM

For more information on **Gian Michael Simmons Productions**, projects, groups, writing and poetry samples, and **Love Liberates Inc. Nonprofit**. Also on the website, over 200 products including clothing, coats, face masks, posters, hats, bags, and more! Member Reward Program for points on spending, member coupons, and **Free Worldwide Shipping.**

Gian is also working on a subscription-based podcast channel, newsletter, and expanding social media groups and podcasts. Everything from faith, poetry, music, teaching essential skills, financial literacy, events, networking, and more. Stay tuned. You may **become a free member** of my personal website for exclusive-member content and **download the free Spaces by Wix app** for a personalized experience.

FROM THE AUTHOR

My name is Gian Michael Simmons and I will be your host. I will be accompanying you on this journey to the quiet place found deep within. It is there that you will uncover life's hidden meanings and purpose. It is my goal that you quiet the noise, discover the sounds of silence, and experience the true power of love. The journey of Silence Speaks is available in four volumes. Be sure to get a copy of each volume.

I will be personally escorting you on this journey. I decided to write this book and share the story of Life and Love through the engagements of words and characters. I wanted to be the voice of the voiceless. The voice of the many unspoken and, often, forgotten. I challenge you to search your life and search your soul. May you find that Silence Speaks. May you discover the true power of love. I Speak Life and I Speak Love For You. Be Healed. Be Delivered. Be Set Free. Allow me to take you on a interplanetary journey beyond asteroids, stars, and planets. May this journey take you to a quiet place where the winds don't blow. Let it allow you to hear your own voice and the voice of your higher self. From the homeless to the rich and famous, you will hear your stories. My goal was to share stories that transcended across all ages, races, cultures, sex, and classes. I interviewed homeless people and many professionals. I heard their stories and wanted to share them with the world. In their stories, may you discover that We Are One and that no human being can be any more or less human than the next. In spite of our individual circumstances, We Are One.

I write daily and very often. I have been writing and speaking, on a national level, since I was in the fifth grade. When I was 10 years old, I represented New York State and the nation at the White House. I wrote a speech and presented the Late New York State Governor Mario Cuomo with an award the we made for him in arts class. I also presented my poem I wrote and speech at the event. This event was very important because we were celebrating my school, and others, becoming a magnet school. Magnet schools were established, after the Civil Rights Movement, to promote diversity and equality in the education system. Being a part of history would later reveal my true gift. I became a orator of words and a true King of Hearts.

As I matured and aged, I developed an affinity for words. I also enjoyed reading, writing, and public speaking. I began to nurture my talents. I became a student of words and characters. I study their meanings and engagements. I appreciate their rich meaning and divine significance. I would read the dictionary, daily, and learn new words. I love to challenge myself with learning. I became fascinated by books. As a child, I would ask my mother to buy me books and art supplies as gifts instead of toys and video games. I was always writing and creating things. My creativity matured to a level whereby I mastered the art of discipline. That was my way of having fun as a child and even as an adult. I was tested as a genius in elementary school.

My writing talents and skills would land me an opportunity to write for the local newspaper. I had written several published articles when I was only thirteen years old and worked with them for two years. Writing is very natural to me. It would amaze you to know that many of my poems and writings were written within minutes and most of them requiring very little editing. It's like I hear messages, songs, and poetry all day. I hear the smallest details. I am very spiritually grounded. I am very connected with heaven. Musical and poetic seeds are divinely sown in me daily. These seeds I sow in the people. I speak to you. I speak for you. I love you. I am you. Make your life interplanetary and travel, with me, to the place where Silence Speaks.

The time has come to speak to the hearts and minds of Earth's inhabitants to encourage love, peace, and unity, To end the destruction of relationships and to remind us that We Are One.

Silence Speaks will be available in four volumes and released on the same day.

This book will highlight areas in personal development, inter-personal relationships, leadership, faith, Spirituality, motivation, strength, and character.

I am also a student of history and knowledge. I am a seeker of wisdom and higher truth. Before man was able to write, knowledge and history was passed through verbally through spoken words, poetic forms, and songs. Silence Speaks engages in this approach and I hope that you discover its rich and deep meaning.

I wrote Silence Speaks for all those that live amongst us and call ourselves human, including ourselves. This book is for all those that know that they are human and inhabit the earth but wonder where, in the world, did I come from? They live amongst us. They're even in our body. In fact, when we look ourselves in the mirror, something extra-terrestrial is looking right at them. Sometimes we wonder, not only where did I come from, but if I am human at all. We live amongst each other. We breathe the same air. May we uncover the commonality and oneness of all.

The time has come for man to abandon his destructive and wicked ways. To depart from wickedness and evil. To end corruption and violence. To end inequalities. To end injustice. To return Love into hearts, minds, and actions. To raise the consciousness. We are love. We are a product of love's imagination morphed into matter. May we restore the hope and love for all. We are One.

౧ఌ ౖ౨ఌ

THE CALL FOR THE SILENCE SPEAKS SERIES OVERVIEW: FEATURED IN ALL SERIES

Humbly submitted and released into this earthly realm, sacred and powerful messages echoing from eternity, through the ages, speaking unconditional love. Love that's anchored on the sacred, eternal and undying faith, not just faith in a higher power, but true consciousness; Oneness. Since the universal consciousness exists outside of space and time, everything in space and time are connected. Nothing is divided or separated. We must, thus, return to this state of individual Oneness to discover that, with love, all things are possible.

We must examine the things that divide us, such as privilege and return to the self-made man and woman. By self-made men, I mean precisely what the phrase imparts to the popular mind. They are the men who, without the ordinary help and favoring circumstances which usually distinguish and promote success, have risen, in one way or another and attained knowledge, wisdom, power, position, and fame in the world.

They are the men who owe very little to birth, relationships, or friendly surroundings. They have neither had the advantage of wealth inherited, nor early training, nor approved means of education. Like the overtaxed Hebrew slaves of Egypt, they have been required to make bricks without straw. They are the men and women who have come up, not only without the voluntary aid and assistance of society, but often in open, direct and derisive defiance of all powers and efforts of society to obstruct, repress, and keep them down. They were purposed into creation to love, inspire, motivate, build, engineer and stretch out the curtains of man's habitations and usher mankind into the very cradle of embracing our Divine Purpose, Rights, and Gifts as Eternal Sons and Daughters of Love; hence, created by Love to afford mankind with the powers and abilities to experience life abundantly and navigate the endless fountains of living waters which flows out of the hearts of true believers.

They are the men that time couldn't defeat or trap. They mastered their skills, talents, and abilities to soar like Eagles and embrace realms of existence whereby time is timeless. In a world of schools, colleges, and other institutions of learning, they have been compelled to obtain education out of fire, air, earth, and water. In a peculiar sense, they are indebted to themselves for themselves and are architects of their own fortunes.

Creatures of Love, thereby inheriting the true powers of love to be creators and sustainers of Life. If they have traveled far, they have made the road on which they traveled. If they have ascended high, they have built their own ladder. Flying, without wings, like eagles soaring beyond earthly realms and heights. Questing without bounds. Seeking and Finding.

They are the men who come from fathomless social depths and have burst the social strata that bound them; like roses that grew from concrete and not wounded or defeated by the thorns masked behind the beauty of the rose pedals. From the cornfield, the plow, and the workbench, from the heartless pavements of large and over crowded cities, barefoot, hungry, and friendless, out of the depths, obscurity, darkness, and destitution, they have come. Flung overboard in the midnight storm, on a perilous ocean, without oars, ropes, or life-preservers, they have bravely buffeted the frowning billows with their own sinewy arms, and have risen in safety, where other men, supplied with the best appliances, have fainted, despaired and gone down.

Such men as these, whether we find them in one position or another, whether in the college or in the factory, whether professors or plowmen, whether of Anglo-Saxon or Anglo-African origin, are self-made men, and have fairly won that title, and what honor soever that title implies.

We stand at a time where we must find love. I am certain, however, if the people are provided with more pure water, enriched with essential nutrients and vitamins, they will be afforded with the opportunity to regain the substance and inner-strengths to deter from their destructive and deadly ways and chose to embrace love. Man's purpose is to stretch out their curtains and tents of their habitations, strengthening the stakes, and filling desolate cities, nations, and hearts with the strongest elements known to man; that being Love and Water, uncontaminated and abundantly flowing with living water and not still-water that emits horrible scents like the rotten meat from the many dreams deferred. We need more substantive efforts and more attempts to bring Love back to her rightful place in the hearts, minds, and actions of the people. Questing without bounds, seeking and we shall find, knocking and doors will be opened and we shall find Love perched on the very fire escapes of people's souls. Souls so wounded and battered to, whereby, they have pledged lives anchored on fears, ignorance, and destruction. It's said that the house is where the heart resides, thus we say a house is a heart of love. People so wounded, hearts so heavily accumulated and polluted with toxicity, souls carrying the frozen and heavy load arriving at an existence whereby people are living lives far less-than what we were created and purposed to live. So heavily soiled in fears, doubts, hurts, and pains that they are so afraid to enter their own homes. That they are, in essence, living on the fire escapes of their souls; living partial, if any, real living life or living palliatively. Forgotten that the cold and broken still have a hallelujah.

Yes, Love, herself can be saved and it's not too late to parachute her back into the hearts and souls of the living dead. For this day shall we proclaim the return of Love in the fullness, beauty, and true joy of her warm embrace. This day, shall, living waters flow abundantly out the hearts and bellies of the renewed souls that rise and awaken with a new song, a new joy, a renewed commitment to chose Love and Life. And, to accept that they are the head and not the tail. My brothers, my sisters anointed in the many colors and charms the rainbow radiates reminding us of the covenant that we have with Love. We are the very rainbow in sky of Love. Man be healed, delivered, and set free. Not someday, not one day, but Today. All Day. All Day. All the Glory, Honor, and Praise belongs to the Almighty and only the mistakes are ours. Consigning this message to our earthly remains. Sealing it with the Love of the Almighty and the Blood that flows from man to man. Let us see love and marvel at her beauty; the sun that radiates and rises with each stride of her step and as she smiles upon us may we continue to share the water that she bathes us with. May we wash away every harmful waste and accumulation of anything toxic. May

we deal one great death blow to this destruction man
has embraced and may we LOVE LIVE LOVE.

Fire in my belly
I can't sleep
When I quiet the noise
The universe speaks to me
Sounds that would bewilder the common mind
Channeling of unspoken wisdom
The unfolding of time
The conclave with the Father
Nurtured by Mother
Who promised you tomorrow?

Silence Speaks

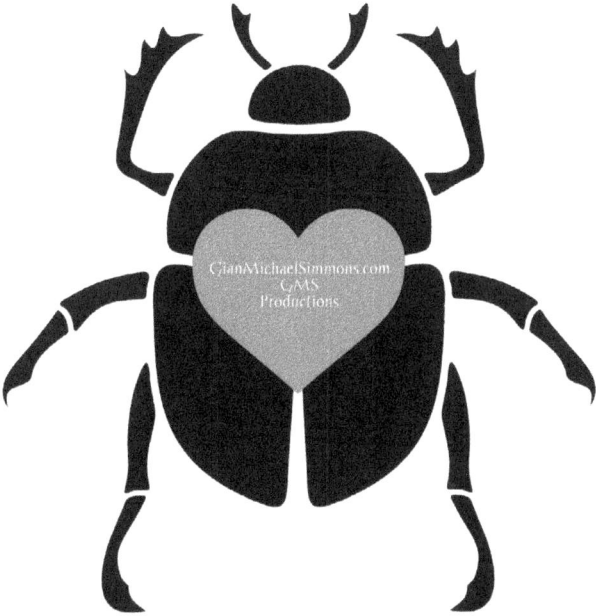

BE SURE TO BUY ALL FOUR VOLUMES OF
SILENCE SPEAKS

WELCOME

Look within your heart
You shall see
You'll finally be a piece of me

Trapped deep within the soul
You will know
What you mean to me

So
Search your life
Search your soul
Just draw me close to thee

Let love be the air of your skies
The wings of your life
Heart and soul will be free

The four doors to your soul
Let love be your guide to thee

Bring self to whole
Let love walk your stride
Hearts keys of love you will find

Gian Michael Simmons

So
Close your eyes
Conquer your mind
Because
Love can't be stopped
Love can't be unfound
Love is all we know

Welcome

DID YOU READ SILENCE SPEAKS?

Silence has spoken
You're still praying to Jesus
Too busy saying Amen
You need to read Silence Speaks
You really need to think again

I knocked on heaven's door
Broke through the door
Just to pass you the key
You'd rather live trapped
Crying to be free

Release the chains of
Slavery

You need to change your
Thoughts
Actions
History

Think about your children
Time
Legacy

Look at what you're doing to you
Look at what you're doing to me

I dropped hidden knowledge
Lost
Once forbidden
Mental Surgery

Translate what's hidden
Freely

Hid it behind those words
Masked it behind those characters
You need to find you
You need to find me
Sailing through the hands of time
Spit like
Poetry

How about you plant those thoughts
Sow
Grow a
Tree

I know you like that flow
I know how you like it to
Be

The King Of Hearts
I'll
BE

Vesting the spirit
Evaporating the flesh
Challenging the mind
Putting souls to the test

Traveling lonely highways
Speaking through time
Gingerly

Just as Ancient Waters, I'll
BE

Passing you some water
Generously

Be sure to fill your cup
Completely

Before you put my book down
Tell Someone
Love
Share a
Tree

We can save
Mother Earth if
WE

Get into the Silence
Hear her Speak
Softly

Did You Read My Book
Silence Speaks

Buy Silence Speaks
Volumes I, II, III and IV

MY DAILY PRAYER

Mercy saw me
Not for who I am, but for who I was created to
    be
I was created with purpose
Love is the way, the truth, and the light
I thank you for my life

I give my all to thee
You'll be the one who sets me free
And my heart and soul says yes
Prepare my heart so that I can serve you
Heal my mind and make my complete
I'm available to you
Use me as you will
I submit my will to your will

I give my all to thee
Set my soul free
And make me completely and freely yours
This is my humble prayer
I pray for forgiveness of my failures, shortcom-
    ings, and mistakes

Gian Michael Simmons

Keep me in your love
Your love liberates
I belong to you
I will be what and who you created me to be
More than a conqueror
In all things, I give you thanks
I thank you for my life

WHAT'S YOUR LIFE BLUEPRINT?

One must pose this question: What principles and formulas dictate, regulate, and govern the cores of your thoughts, actions, inactions, beliefs, and values? Reality is that many of us are only operating on the surface and very few have penetrated beyond the skin and flesh. Mathematics, science, physics, astrology, psychology, and other disciplines all exist as vessels to sail our ships afloat natural balance of peace, harmony, love, equilibrium.

Today, I challenge you to release and abandon the shackles of excuses and flaws that limit and restrict your ability to thrive and succeed. In your life's blueprint, may it be completely void of excuses. Let no obstacle or challenge stop you from achieving the greatness you were created to be.

What will tomorrow's future say about the present you? Will your name be included in the vocabulary and engagements of words and conversations? Would you be a subject of discussion or just a topic? What realms of space

would your life's blueprints transcend and engulf?
What would eternity speak of thee?

What would you say to tomorrow if you
spoke to it today?
When you vision the future what do you see?
Let the future You talk to the present You, today

"**We must learn how to lose ourselves in**
order to be who we were meant to be"
- Gian Michael Simmons

REAL ESTATE

The best real estate you can invest in is your mind
You'll never run out of space
You'll never have to find the time
You'll never have to worry about fluctuating prices
And, it pays income all the time
Payments are never late
Most time, they arrive early

Best thing
It's free

You'd require few renovations
You'd need few repairs
Your construction will last forever
If truth is what you seek
Let true knowledge be your life's blueprint
Let love be it's foundation

DARK CHOCOLATE

I guess that's why they say
Put a piece of dark chocolate
Under your tongue
Enlighten your mind

Because
The truth is really dark
Bitter Sweet

It's good for your body
But
You may not find it to be sweet

You may not like the truth
May not like the taste
May not understand the flavor
You may not hear the sound
May not sense the Savior

Too busy
Lost in what's syrupy
Stuck on that high fructose

Silence Speaks

Focusing on what's sweet
Forgotten what's good for your body
So, your life is incomplete

Next time you eat chocolate
Make sure it's at least 80% cocoa
You may not find it to be sweet
In reality, it is
Truth is always sweet

Dark Chocolate

LEARN HOW TO FLY

I went left and I went right
The thoughts in my mind keep me up at night
Sometimes, I toss and turn but I
I learned how to fight

Sometimes I fell
Most times I stood
I had to get my life up out the hood
Look at me crazy
I wish you would
Give me a try

Sometimes the winds just seems to blow
Sometimes the streams take me where I
    shouldn't go
But I learned how to fly

A day will come when crimes of man
Dark as the night
But I still stand
I learned how to fly

COMPOUND

COMPOUND
One plus one, let's compound, together,
get through this wrath
Add those digits up,
Come together, yup
Calculate that math
Stack the paper, yup
Over flow your cup

Sow thy daily bread
Exercise compounding might,
Now your money is right
Rest in designers bed 🛏
All night

Caution your spending, put away stacks and stacks
Because, there will come a day, bills, back to backs
Keep your money green, no fade to black
Because black is so red, now your money is dead
Just remember what I said,
Compound, Compound
Overflow your cup and take, thee, thy daily bread
I hope my words encouragement and I hope my
words fed

Gian Michael Simmons

Master the art of compound interest
COMPOUND   COMPOUND   COMPOUND
GIAN MICHAEL SIMMONS
ঌ

ৎ৴৽ ৵৽৵

FOUR DOORS

Come and knock on the door
Love is calling you
Been through this time and time before
You say, three company too

You still waving at them walls
Lifting up those curtains
Bouncing on four doors
Jumping on your soul
Trying to get through them doors

Bouncy
Tipsy
Gravy
Wavy

You
Twist
You
Turn

You
Bounce
You
Thrill

Seeking that
Touch
Feel
Chill

Knock on those
Four Doors

Greet your
Hello

Sing praises to the Spirit
Bring oneness with the soul

Break through those doors

THE VOICE

Hear the Voice
Inside
You hear it
But
You question
You

You think you're going
Crazy
Insane
You
Think you're talking to yourself
In reality you are
A higher self
Than who you're used to

Distracted by the noise outside
You ignore the Voice within
Too busy talking with others
Missing the real Voice you should be talking with

Ignoring the calls from silence
Silencing the calls
The calls from the Voice

Gian Michael Simmons

You should hear
It's silent
But loud
Don't you fear
The Voice

THE CHANGE

What if my check
Forgot to pay
Leaving my money
Bouncing like basketballs

Dribble
Dribble

Bounce
Bounce

The money that's there
Noisy pocket change
No silent paper
To quiet the bounce
Just a bunch of change
Making noise
It just won't stop

But, I gotta stay on my grind
Trying to get to the real cash
Gotta get that paper

Gian Michael Simmons

Convert that currency
Quiet the noise
The Change

SING ALONG

Children of the world
You can be anyone that you wish to be
May your dreams flow like rivers
May love be the flag your ship sails upon
May you conquer your seas

Sing along
Sing along
Children
Bring your love, laughter, and all

Sing along
Sing along
Children
Come to that place where you belong

Sing Along
Sing Along
Children
Love will take you that place called home

Sing Along
Dream Along
Children

ILLUMINATE

Men playing as God
Humble yourselves, Come to me, The Almighty
    said
It's time to let our lights shine
Bring love back, rise man from dead

Man's trapped in times
Spending paper, chasing dimes
Too much sex in bed

Lost in fables
Truth trapped in stables
Propaganda locked on cables
Music and Science lead

So, you go to church
All day, all night, kneel and pray to God
What God is He?
She?
Mans Bible, The Word read

Illuminate your lights
Shine so bright

Find the truth inside
Love hearts wide opened, but tight
Love said

ILLUMINATE
THE ONE

ALIEN

I'm pushing through Earth's Lands
Building Towers
Ancient Pyramid lands
I don't make a sound
Buy a vowel

Mysteries that'll blow your mind
The time is the hour
Living in Darkness
Enlighten your mind

Can you see
What I see
Calling me Alien
Like that's my name

They used to call me Sci-Fi
Because I fly high
In the galaxy
And, I dance around the stars
You call me a Alien

TIMES ARE CHANGING

It's like man is on the brink of extinction
Man's too busy driving around town in a Lincoln
Tell, Tell, Tell
Catch, Catch, Catch
Lies Lies
Lies

Buried truths trapped in layers upon layers,
    eyes so blind

They think they can save man all by themselves
So, they stacked their hearts on kitchen shelves

This is true
Locks, Bolts
Nuts and Screws
This we know
Reach deep inside
Let the Spirit Glow

Life is like a stock
Temperature rising
Voluminous favor

I got my eyes on my Savior
I got my eyes on Freedom

Love bring you up, life brings you down
Private share offering, cap and gown
Ain't life amazing when you smile through your
    frown
Because, the times are changing

Wake up your eyes, open your heart, set love
    free
There's a time in your life
Where you must rise and stand
Guide your feet, let the Light hold your hand

You shall make it
You shall drink from love's waters
Let it quench your thirst
Because, the times are changing

LIFE

From the day that earthlings were morphed
    into matter
Souls seeking to conquer the lands
Earthlings danced through the sun
The bulls run high through the endless skies
Carrying dreams so far into the endless times
Earthlings came from beyond a star

Come sideways
Come fatter
I see through the Chi Chi Chi
Chatter

I travel on asteroids and stars
Let it amortize your mind to see through the
    soul
Gods traveling to Earth searching for gold

Life moving through circles
And it moves the stars
Eagle eye view of the sparrow
Through faith and love
Til we find that place
Where times unwinding

In Earth's darkest hour
In cosmic turbulent despair
Poverty, miseducation, false religions, wide-
    spread violence
Do you care?
Will you be there?

Fatherless son
Motherless daughter
Heavy hearted husband
Wounded spirit woman
Abused and confused little boys and girls
Do you care?
Will you be there?
Life

WHY CAN'T WE BE FRIENDS?

You better not blink
Drink drink drink
Let's take it again from the top

Drink it fast
Drink it slow
Swallow
You better not blow

Heads moving so fast
Now, my head is spinning
Getting a head all day
Feels like
I'm Winning

Sometimes
When you win
It feels like you lose
So
I'd rather call it a truce

Why Can't We Be Friends?

Gian Michael Simmons

Together
We could conquer the world
I Love You
Because
You bring out the best in me
We have a lot in common
More than you think

My head's moving fast
I'm getting a head
I can't even think
Drink drink drink
Through your ill feelings down the kitchen sink

Why can't we be friends?

SPIRIT VS. MATTER

You say
Dimension
I say
Density
You say
Ladders
Jacob's Ladder
Lack true courage
Insecurity

Chutes and Ladders
Quantum Physics
Instigate Me

Lost in math
Studying the path
Sacred Geometry

Now it's
Spirit Vs. Matter

Music to the chatter
Mind pop locking
All you hear is the latter

Gian Michael Simmons

Ringtone your thoughts
Climbing down the ladder
All you see is matter

The truth I seek
Is buried in the waters
Sailing upon
Shoreless seas

It's a raging war
Spirit Vs. Matter

FIGHT

There comes a time in your life
When you must do what is right
You must reach deep inside
Let Love and Peace be your guide

Stand tall through it all
Rise and stand, you shall not fall
Thick and through it all
You must Fight

When you're filled with pain
Fight
Through your Tears and rain
Fight
When there's nothing to gain
Fight
Let peace be your friend

Deep in your heart you shall find
A peace that endures lifetimes
A joy that your soul shall see
May the spirit of life be free

You
Just **Fight**

Be prepared for time moves like a lion
Be prepared for time moves through the paths
Be prepared for the time falls before you
Be prepared

*"The man or woman that stands and fights
one more round never falls"*
- Gian Michael Simmons
You Must Fight

SPACESHIP

Close your eyes
Get into the silence
Pay Attention
Witness

There's a spaceship
Awaiting
Listen

It's Golden
Shiny
Can't you see

It'll take you past
Stars, Planets, Galaxies
Mysteries
Miracles Unseen

If you try to see it with your eyes
You may not see it
If you try to hear it with your ears
You may not hear it

Gian Michael Simmons

Close your eyes
Silence
Lift-Off
Spaceship

FOLLOW

First, I Gave You Silence
Then, I Let Silence Speak
Now, I Gave You Some Love
But, The Journey Is Not Complete

Be Sure To Follow
Be Sure To Stay Tuned
Be Sure To Bring A Friend

Be Sure To Find You
Be Sure To Find Me
Enlighten Your Journey

Lighten Up Your Path
Bring Wrath To The Darkness
Be Prepared For The Wrath
Make Sure That You
Get Into The Math

1+1
Is Falling
We Need To Hear The Sounds Of Love
Love Is Calling

1+1
Come Together
Do The Math

Follow
Your Heart

Follow
Gian Michael Simmons
The King Of Hearts
Brighten Up Your Path
Love Is Calling
Follow

Follow @ GianMichaelSimmons on all social media platforms/www.gianmichaelsimmons.com

PRODIGAL SONS

Born left of the prism of our ancestry shade
We are gods lost within ourselves
Swinging to the melodic beats of pendulum times
Chasing the illusions of a distorted reality
Man marvels at the vastness of eternity
Just to only see stars

The journey from One to Man back to One
3D
Third Dimension Living
The created man
The Adam
Live and breathing sacred corpses
Seeking the Everlasting Breath of Eternal Life
To complete the journey of man
And return back to the Holy One

Flaming spirits carrying the burdens of frozen truths
Truths melting at zero degrees
Besides man's trapped in time
Locked away under the firmament
Roaming dry lands surrounded by living waters

Gian Michael Simmons

Terrestrial living resorting to gazing at stars
Trying to be planets
Prodigal sons of the Forgotten One

∽∾

ANCIENT WATERS

What an Ocean
Precious seas lay ahead
As I sail the waters of life
Rivers lead to freedom

For Your Glory
I'll cherish the flowing of the tides
To see Your Face
Amazing Grace
This is my song to you
I Sing to you
My Heart cries out for Freedom
For Your Glory
This is my song I sing to you, as your child
Embrace me in Your Arms of Love
May the stream's flow, the river's flow, the
ocean's flow, The water's flow
Lead me to Your Love

MOTHER NATURE

I Give LIFE
Without ME

You are nothing

But
You're Killing Me

POLLUTION
On The Lands
And In The Seas

The Trees
I Give To Breathe
You BURN

The WATERS
To Drink
You TOUCH and TURN

You Spread Wickedness In My Skies
Destructive Weapons
Chem Trails

Confusing The Mind
Chaos

Now
Plants Eating Animals

The Animals Are Going
Extinct

I RAISE Volcanoes To Make you
THINK

Remember Golden Lands Under Water Before
They
SINK

WATCH your Bridges
Major Cities
Get READY For
Shark Tank

I Send My Birds With The Voice Of Heaven
Birds Flying With No Trees To
Land
You Can't Hear Heavenly Songs
It Won't Be Long

Gian Michael Simmons

Before

I Raise

Deadly Seas
Hurricanes
Waters Overflow lands
Evaporate you
Desert your lands
Before you
Blink

I Provide What You Need
It's NEVER Enough
You're Always Exploring

Constantly Digging In My Body
Seeking My Treasures
Spoiling My Goods
Seeking Life's Pleasures

You Think What's Mine Is yours
You're Sadly Mistaken
There's Levels To This
I'm The One Who Can Put You On Course For
Extinction

Silence Speaks

I Give you Free Energy
You Keep Distorting
I Raise Crop Circles
I Give you Facts
Misinformation you Keep Reporting

You accepted a nature other than your own
Labeled it Human Nature
You may be human and all
Call It What You Like

You Think you can destroy Me
I'll Annihilate you
I'll Raise The Waters
Wash Away Every Memory OF you
ERASE you
I'M MOTHER NATURE

FATHER IS HURTING

Father is crying
She's hurting
We see rain, storms, clouds
Lightening
We hear Thunder

Her children have forgotten her

She hid them in the bellies of living planets
Even some, she hid deep in the seas
She's raging through the stars
She's dancing through the heavens
She's moving through the seas

Wedding Ceremony
Holy Matrimony

The marriage she would grow to regret
Having babies with the Tree of Life
Father Time devouring her kids
Eating her babies
Stealing her Thunder

Makes you wonder

It's the mystery of antiquity

It's your herstory
When the heavens came falling down

On Earth
A Shell was placed around her kids
To protect them from dark heavens

Her Spirit
She masked in Nature and implanted within us
Her belly
She stretched out and made inhabitable lands
Her limbs
She positioned as trees
Stretching all throughout the Earth
Her roots
She planted as ancient forests nestled in the
    wilderness
Her veins
Are the minerals that provide for substance
Her blood
The blood in her veins keeps us connected as
    One
Fuels our transportation

Her eyes
Light the heavens and earths
Provide guidance and light
Her angels are always in the skies
Watching over us

Amongst other things
We see
Commodities
Birds, stars, and planets

Although the sun shines
It's an illusion to the true light
The Light that shines within
She's hidden herself deep in space
Deep in the soul
Hidden deep in dark matter
Setting the tone
Guarding The Throne
Until we gather to the place
Where we belong

If you get into the **Silence**
You'll hear her **Speak**
You'll hear her tone

Some of her children
Grew into giants, monsters, and beasts

Silence Speaks

Some fell in Spirit
Some faded as ghosts
Some have passed on
Some are lost
Buried deep in the seas
Some are trapped deep in the lands
Some are invisible

Those on Earth
Grew up in hell
Not far from heaven

Children eating her bread
Plants and animals harvesting her lands
Men toiling her Spirit
Capturing souls
Destroying her body
Father is hurting

Will you hear her cry
Do you feel her pain
Or will you pass on by
Father is hurting

SHINING FOR YOU

So Greater
Is The Love You Give
No Matter How Much I Love
Nothing Compares
To Your Love

You Give
The Sun
The Moon
The Stars
The Horizon
The Ocean Floors

I Give
My All
To You
And
So Much More

I'll Keep Shining For You
Just As Bright As The Love You Give
Nothing Compares
You're Always There
Showing You Care

I'm Shining For You

You Mean The World To Me
Before I Was Born
You Chose Me
To Live
To Love
To Rise
To Conquer

I'm Shining For You

SILENCE SPEAKS

Sometimes the silence makes a sound
Creating contradicting realties in this dreamlike world
Where anything is possible
In the deep
Space

Thoughts
Vibrations
Words and thoughts morphed into characters and
sounds
Creating

Consciousness
Being tested in this dreamlike state of existence
Guess that's why they say perception is not always
reality

The knowledge of good and evil
The will of The Almighty
Spectacles of star dust traveling time

This body of mine in the waters of life
Time traveling

So, should I stop hearing and listen?
Or stop listening and hear?

I guess that's why the pain of death inhabits the eyes
To look deep within the soul
Rebirth
And hear the Voice in silence
For even **Silence Speaks**

❧ ❧

The Time Has Come To Seek A Higher Truth Other Than Faith
Faith Without <u>Works</u> Is Dead

<u>The movement has begun</u>! **Silence Speaks Love Liberates**

Silence Speaks and **Love Liberates** are movements combined with business projects and followed by a Multi-Book-Volume Series, over 100 pages in each volume, to connect you with God. **Silence Speaks Jesus Saves book is a standalone book and not a series volume book.** The series are designed for one to read in any order, as each multi-dimensional book has a different focus matter of discussion and flows with the overall theme of Silence Speaks and Love Liberates. For committed and advanced readers, you may read the series in the order as follows as each following volume presents a journey to God and additional aroma to the **<u>feature books, which are highlight books for all readers</u>. The feature book for Gian Michael Simmons Productions is "Silence Speaks Jesus Saves".** <u>I would highly suggest that all to read this volume</u>. **For the Silence Speaks Volume Series, the feature book** is **Silence Speaks Volume Seven: I AM THAT I AM, Gian Michael Simmons.** Again, all books may be read in any order. The focus and contents of each book may be found in each book description. Additionally, all projects are described in mission statements.

Repent. Seek ye the kingdom of heaven is at hand Jesus holds the keys to salvation

Available on Amazon books, Apple Books, Barnes and Nobles on Paperback and E-Book versions. E-Books also on my website

Silence Speaks Jesus Saves

Silence Speaks Volume Collection

1. Volume One: Life
2. Volume Two: Love
3. Volume Three: Consciousness
4. Volume Four: The Motivation
5. Volume Five: College, The Garden of Life
6. Volume Six: Silence Speaks Jesus Saves ate it!
7. Volume Seven: I AM THAT I AM, Gian Michael Simmons

Love Liberates Volume Collection

1. Volume One: Black Poetry
2. Volume Two: Pretty Girls

www.ingramcontent.com/pod-product-compliance
Lightning Source LLC
Chambersburg PA
CBHW060416050426
42449CB00009B/1981